IF I REALLY WANTED TO

BE A GREAT FRIEND

I WOULD . . .

RACINE, WI

If I Really Wanted to Be a Great Friend, I Would . . .
ISBN: 979-8-88898-105-4 - *Paperback*
ISBN: 979-8-88898-106-1 - *Hardcover*
ISBN: 979-8-88898-107-8 - *Ebook*
Copyright © 2023 by Honor Books
Racine, WI

Cover design, interior design, and editing by Faille Schmitz. Manuscript prepared by Rachel St. John Gilbert, Atlanta, Georgia.

INTRODUCTION

Many people take friendship for granted. But true friendship is difficult to find and even more difficult to keep. It has been said that in a lifetime, it would be extraordinary for a person to have acquired five real friends. That's right. Five individuals who are willing to stick it out through the years—sharing your sorrows and joys, taking the good with the bad, forgiving and being forgiven.

The simple insights contained in this small book can't guarantee you a circle of loving, caring, lifelong friends—nothing can! What they can do is help you understand the principles of friendship so you can become a better friend yourself. Being a good friend is really the key to having good friends.

God bless you as you pursue the precious gift of friendship.

IF I REALLY WANTED TO
BE A GREAT FRIEND,
I WOULD . . .

BE HOSPITABLE

Hospitality is a concept that seems old fashioned in our fast-paced, self-oriented world. Webster's defines it as "generous and cordial reception; ready reception." After a long, hard day at the office, being hospitable sounds like a tall order, doesn't it? Just the same, laying out the welcome mat can be an incredible gift to someone who is lonely or new in the community. It's a kind gesture for the friends you already have.

Being hospitable will serve to solidify current friendships and help you initiate new ones. And most people won't care if you live in a grand mansion or a tiny apartment. They just know it feels good to be welcomed into your home and into your life.

Offer hospitality to one another without grumbling.

1 PETER 4:9

IF I REALLY WANTED TO
BE A GREAT FRIEND,
I WOULD . . .

LEARN TO

KEEP

CONFIDENCES

THE TRUST OF A FRIEND IS A TERRIBLE THING TO WASTE.

One of the primary benefits of true friendship is having the freedom to share our deepest thoughts. This requires a listener who not only hears but also keeps confidences. We all desire to have friends—at least one—with whom we can feel safe. The word confidential is even derived from the root word confidence.

Learn to put a lock on your lips and keep secrets secret. When you feel the compulsion to reveal what you've been told—and you will—remember that trust builds relationships and betrayal tears them apart. Show that you are trustworthy and expect to receive trust in return.

The human heart has hidden treasures,
In secret kept, and silence sealed.

CHARLOTTE BRONTE

Greet Friends with Genuine Enthusiasm

FRIENDLINESS IS CONTAGIOUS—START AN EPIDEMIC.

Have you ever met someone for the first time and been impressed by the way they greeted you with a warm smile, an enthusiastic "hello!" and a question or two about how you're doing? Isn't it interesting how special a little focused attention like that can make you feel?

Life shouldn't be so harried that we don't have time to be genuinely friendly. Why not make it a point to greet your friends regularly with a kind countenance, a warm welcome, and an expressed interest in their well-being? A little kindness brightens everyone's day, and it's a considerate way to reach out to friends each time you see them.

A man that hath friends must shew himself friendly.

PROVERBS 18:24 KJV

IF I REALLY WANTED TO
BE A GREAT FRIEND,
I WOULD . . .

KEEP
SHORT
ACCOUNTS

DON'T MAJOR ON THE MINORS.

With so many varied and unique personalities roaming around this earth, it's inevitable that our friendships will hit some bumps along the way. Good friends realize that everyone has shortcomings and are willing to forgive and forget—in a split second whenever possible.

Make a point to downplay touchy situations that occasionally arise. The old saying, "Don't make a mountain out of a mole hill," is a good adage to keep in mind. Strive to be humble and realize that everyone has faults. It's much more important to keep your friendships on good terms than to be proven "right."

To err is human, to forgive divine.

ALEXANDER POPE

IF I REALLY WANTED TO
BE A GREAT FRIEND,
I WOULD . . .

BELIEVE THE BEST OF PEOPLE

BEFORE DOUBTING, GIVE FRIENDS THE BENEFIT OF THE DOUBT.

We human beings tend to see life through a narrow perspective. What we need is a bit of peripheral vision. For example, when plans we have made with a friend go awry, our tendency would be to take the situation personally or totally analyze it, drawing conclusions before we have a clear understanding of what actually transpired.

When faced with a friend's action or lack of action in a certain situation, pretend you're an unbiased detective. Wait until you get the facts from your friend before thinking the worst. Open your mind to the possibility that there were unavoidable circumstances that had nothing to do with ill feelings toward you.

In spite of everything I still believe that people are really good at heart.

ANNE FRANK

IF I REALLY WANTED TO
BE A GREAT FRIEND,
I WOULD . . .

LOOK FOR WHAT I CAN GIVE

FRIENDSHIPS RIDE IN THE EBB AND FLOW OF GIVE AND RECEIVE.

F riendship is a two-way street, or at least it should be. Sometimes you will need to call on your friends for help and sometimes they will have to call on you. If you aren't willing to give, you will never have strong, centered friendships.

Take a personal inventory. Ask yourself, "Have I been too busy or distracted to be a reciprocal giver?" If so, make a point to reach out to your friends as soon as possible to keep the momentum of friendship going. When you find yourself on the receiving end, don't forget to be a gracious receiver. Take turns giving and receiving support. That's what friendship is all about.

God loves a cheerful giver.

2 CORINTHIANS 9:7

BE AWARE OF THE POWER OF TOUCH

A SIMPLE HUMAN TOUCH CAN MEAN SO VERY MUCH.

Some people insist, "I'm not a hugger," and we should all be respectful of those boundaries. Yet even a small token of physical affection can make a real impact. Studies have shown that there are undeniable healing properties in physical touch.

We may not be physically ill, but let's face it, it's a tough world out there! We live our lives at a breakneck pace: producing, organizing, giving. What a refreshing, and yes, healing pause a pat on the back, a touch on the arm, or even a quick hug can be. If you're not a "hugging" person, try extending a simple pat on the arm or even a warm handshake. It's a signal of closeness and caring that often results in friendship.

Do not leave my hand without light.

MARC CHAGALL

IF I REALLY WANTED TO
BE A GREAT FRIEND,
I WOULD . . .

GIVE TOKEN GIFTS

H as someone ever given you small gift simply as a token of appreciation for just your being you? It's amazing how a gift that says, "I thought of you when I saw this," can make you feel on top of the world. Consider maintaining a "friendship budget" so that you are free to purchase small gifts of affection or appreciation when you see something that would be perfect for a friend.

These special gifts are a great investment in a relationship. Each time your friend sees the item, chosen expressly for him or her, it will serve as a reminder not only that you care but also that you know and appreciate that person's unique taste, style, and desires.

Liberality consists less in giving a great deal than in gifts well timed.

JEAN DE LA BRUYERE

IF I REALLY WANTED TO
BE A GREAT FRIEND,
I WOULD . . .

LEARN TO COMPLIMENT PEOPLE

IF YOU CAN'T THINK OF SOMETHING NICE TO SAY, THINK HARDER.

Who doesn't love to hear complimentary words? Talk about music to your ears! For some reason, enthusiasm and compliments tend to be given to children more often than adults. And although children need compliments and encouragement, adults do too.

When you think about it, adults are constantly in motion, often doing things for others—whether it's at work, home, church, a club, or elsewhere. So it's important to pause and remember to thank and encourage our friends in their daily lives. Someone once said, "I can live a whole week on one compliment." Go ahead, make your friend's week.

Pleasant words are a honeycomb, sweet to the soul and healing to the bones.

PROVERBS 16:24

IF I REALLY WANTED TO
BE A GREAT FRIEND,
I WOULD . . .

BECOME AN ACTIVE LISTENER

Make like an ear and hear.

We live with such constant stimuli that it's often difficult to focus on one thing at a time. That lack of focus can enter into the arena of our relationships. Yet one of the most thoughtful gifts we can give another human being is our undivided attention. When you fully focus on someone else, you are communicating to them that they are valued—so much so, that you don't want to miss a word they're saying or *how* they're saying it.

Give friends your full attention. Listen without thinking about what you're going to say next. Focus on their eyes, their expressions, their mannerisms—the factors that often speak just as loud as words.

Give every man thy ear, but few thy voice.

William Shakespeare

IF I REALLY WANTED TO
BE A GREAT FRIEND,
I WOULD . . .

BE
VULNERABLE

LET DOWN YOUR GUARD AND REST YOUR HEAD ON THE SHOULDER OF A FRIEND.

Everyone goes through ups and downs. While it's nice to be on an up cycle, encouraging the downtrodden, the reality is no one gets to have it "all together" for very long. We need to take turns being the encourager and the encouraged. Notice how courage is squeezed in the middle of those words. It takes courage to let your guard down and make your needs known.

The next time you're tempted to cover up your discouragement, remember that most people are empathetic to those who are willing to admit they don't have all the answers. Let your friends know that you need their support to make it in this life.

A person's level of security is in direct proportion to his ability to admit his insecurity.

BECKY FREEMAN

IF I REALLY WANTED TO BE A GREAT FRIEND, I WOULD . . .

WRITE NOTES

KEEP IT SIMPLE AND USE THE WRITE STUFF.

E ven if you don't consider yourself a letter writer, you can easily become a note writer. Notes are short and sweet—everyone enjoys receiving them, whether as a surprise in a mailbox or on an office desk.

Be on the lookout for high-quality note cards. You can often find beautiful, creative, or funny notes for less than five dollars a box. Many display reproductions of famous paintings and are like sharing miniature works of art. Use whimsical sealing stickers—from small pressed flowers to fun cartoon characters. Or if you like, you can invest in sealing wax and a seal for a way to add an air of nostalgic elegance.

I have much to write you . . . I hope to see you soon, and we will talk face to face.

3 JOHN 1:13-14

IF I REALLY WANTED TO
BE A GREAT FRIEND,
I WOULD . . .

ASK FOR GOD'S HELP

Ask God to be your Friendship Consultant.

F riends are God's gifts to help us along life's path. They love us, laugh with us, comfort us, and encourage us. If you've ever gone through a period of time when you didn't have friends around you, you've realized how lonely life can feel. Possibly when God allows those lonely seasons, He's teaching us to appreciate the value of a good friend. Maybe He knows we won't casually toss our friends aside at the first sign of discontent if we fully realize that good friends are true treasures.

Ask God to give you a deep appreciation for the friends who decorate your life. Allow Him to show you ways to nurture those relationships. Ask Him to send people your way who need a friend. Then thank Him for the privilege.

True happiness consists not in the multitude of friends, but in the worth and choice.

Ben Jonson

IF I REALLY WANTED TO
BE A GREAT FRIEND,
I WOULD . . .

READ

ABOUT

FRIENDSHIP

LET THE WORDS YOU READ BECOME THE ACTIONS OF YOUR HEART

Many magazines have articles about relationships, and whether it's a "how to" or a true-life story, these can be wonderful ways to sensitize our minds and hearts to the characteristics of great friendships. Books can also be a good source of information and insight into human nature. Browse the shelves at bookstores and the local library.

Daily "flip calendars" are often an inexpensive source of inspiration as we look for reminders that help us become better friends. Many have excerpts from books or an array of thought-provoking quotes. They make nice gifts for your friends too.

There is no accident in our choice of reading.

FRANCOIS MAURIAC

IF I REALLY WANTED TO
BE A GREAT FRIEND,
I WOULD . . .

MAKE MYSELF AVAILABLE TO HELP OUT

DON'T "BEE" TOO BUSY—TAKE TIME TO SHARE SOME HONEY WITH A FRIEND.

Virtually everyone in today's fast-paced society is busy. However, if you want to build friendships, it's important to make yourself available when your friends have occasional needs.

Most people are aware of the busy-ness factor of life and are reluctant to ask for help. The saying, "That's what friends are for!" needs to become as popular in our culture as "I'm so busy!" The investment in a friend's welfare will reap benefits of loyalty and gratefulness, and good friends will want to reciprocate your kindness when you have a need.

A faithful man will be richly blessed.

PROVERBS 28:20

BE
SENSITIVE
TO
SCHEDULES

BE REALISTIC ABOUT DIFFERENCES IN SCHEDULES AND LIFESTYLES.

As we seek to develop friendships, it's good to be aware of lifestyle differences and preferences. We may feel that friendships are a priority and schedule loads of time to spend with our friends. But others may not have the same level of desire for together time.

Some of your friends may have busier schedules, more children, more activities, spouses who work late—factors that can hinder a person's availability. You need not take this personally, but simply ask yourself, "Am I willing to develop this friendship within limited parameters, or am I going to feel frustrated—always looking for more time with this person?" This approach will help you decide whether a certain relationship is worth pursuing.

To live happily with other people one should ask of them only what they can give.

TRISTAN BERNARD

IF I REALLY WANTED TO
BE A GREAT FRIEND,
I WOULD . . .

BE
SENSITIVE
TO
PREFERENCES

FLEXIBILITY AND ACCOMMODATION BRING GROWTH AND APPRECIATION.

F or the young, friendship often means agreeing on everything, dressing alike, looking alike, and loving the same things. But mature friends savor differences. And they have learned to compromise in regard to preferences.

Strive to be flexible whenever possible. Don't always insist that your friend go to the restaurant or movie that is your top pick. Don't expect your friend to always accommodate your schedule or follow your game plan. Be willing to make mutually beneficial compromises for the sake of friendship.

People have one thing in common—they're all different.

ROBERTA S. CULLEY

Be Inquisitive

CARING HEARTS HAVE INQUIRING MINDS.

It's human nature to want to be known, especially by our friends. One of the best ways to get to know someone is simply to ask questions. People are like beautifully wrapped packages, filled with unique treasures, just waiting to be opened and shared with others.

Get into the habit of asking friends leading questions that cannot be answered with yes or no. Pretend you are a skilled interviewer and ask things like, "Wow, that must have been exciting, what were you feeling at the time?" Be grateful for friends who are willing to be known in a deeper way by sharing their thoughts and feelings with you.

"Ask and it will be given to you; seek and you will find; knock and the door will be opened to you."

LUKE 11:9

IF I REALLY WANTED TO
BE A GREAT FRIEND,
I WOULD . . .

LOOK FOR COMMON INTERESTS

If you want to deepen an existing friendship, capitalize on areas of common interest. Long-term compatibility in a friendship needs at least two areas of common interest to develop.

The more important the common interest is to you and the more interests you share, the more likely the friendship will become cohesive. Common circumstances, such as being mothers of children of the same age, can be a strong point. Or perhaps you share an interest in music, art, spiritual beliefs, or certain hobbies. These interests may be what brought you together in the first place. Be sure to focus on them as you watch your friendship grow.

Friendship needs a certain parallelism of life, a community of thought, a rivalry of aim.

HENRY BROOKS ADAMS

If I really wanted to
be a great friend,
I would . . .

Be Willing to
Make the
Introductions

MAKE THE INTRODUCTIONS AND TRUST GOD WITH THE RESULTS.

One of the kindest things you can do for another person is to introduce him or her to your other friends, especially in groups where your friend is a first-time visitor. It's an honor to be introduced into a well-connected group of friends who are willing to embrace another soul and add a new link to their circle of friendship.

Be a gracious friend with a spirit of hospitality. Don't give in to fears that your friends might like your new pal better than they like you (or that they may not like them as well as they like you). Keep an open mind and an open heart. In the end, your kindness is sure to bring you the right kind of friends.

No act of kindness, no matter how small,
is ever wasted.

AESOP

BE SENSITIVE TO THE ISSUE OF CHILDREN

REMEMBER THAT CHILDREN CAN GREATLY IMPACT THE NATURE OF YOUR FRIENDSHIPS.

People with children often have different views of how and how often their kids should be involved when gathering with friends. Whether or not we have children, we need to be aware of friends' expectations.

Children are one of the most precious gifts that God gives us. People usually have very strong feelings about their children and their parenting styles. Parents that have a "hands on" approach may wish to have their children around most of the time. In addition, if the children are younger, there will likely be more distractions in your conversations. Be realistic about your tolerance level when adding children to the friendship equation and make adjustments accordingly.

Sons are a heritage from the Lord, children a reward from him.

PSALM 127:3

IF I REALLY WANTED TO
BE A GREAT FRIEND,
I WOULD . . .

UTILIZE
MODERN
TECHNOLOGY

BECOME A TECHNO-FRIEND.

Many people spend a large amount of time on their home or office computers and smartphones. Thanks to the internet, this can be an easy and natural way to stay connected with a friend. It's an even more powerful tool for keeping in touch if the friend lives some distance from you and you are able to see each other only on occasion.

Your friend can become a pen pal of sorts, and soon you'll be sharing personal thoughts, funny moments in your day, and the ups and downs of life—all of which strengthen intimacy. There are even websites that offer greeting card e-mails that you can send instantaneously to brighten someone's day.

Reading maketh a full man, conference a ready man, and writing an exact man.

FRANCIS BACON

PRACTICE
SPEAKING
POSITIVELY

BE A POSITIVE LIGHT IN THE DARKNESS OF A NEGATIVE WORLD.

It's been said that the default mode of most people's thinking is negative. If we're not aware of it, those negative thoughts can easily turn into negative talk. Take personal inventory. Do you tend to be an optimist or pessimist by nature? Do you tend to think encouraging or discouraging thoughts most of the time?

If you lean toward the pessimistic side, try speaking more positively. Pay attention to your thought patterns and work on reversing negative thinking. Read books or other materials that enhance positive thought patterns. In friendship, negativity can bring others—and the friendship—down.

Keep your sunny side up.

LEW BROWN AND BUDDY DE SYLVA

IF I REALLY WANTED TO
BE A GREAT FRIEND,
I WOULD . . .

BE CAREFUL
NOT TO
CRITICIZE
OTHERS

SPEAK WELL OF FRIEND TO FRIEND—THEY'LL BE WITH YOU TO THE END.

One way to damage a friendship and make other friends wary of your loyalty is to talk negatively about a friend to others. We are imperfect people. As such, we will, at times, become frustrated with one another. If you feel the need to talk out your frustration, avoid doing so in the presence of other friends.

Although your friends might be tempted to chime in with complaints about the frustrating person, they may later wonder if you are talking negatively about them too. This can become an issue of trust. Words are powerful. They will be remembered and can be taken out of context. Be aware of your words and to whom you are speaking, especially when it comes to your friends.

Let your conversation be always full of grace.

COLOSSIANS 4:6

IF I REALLY WANTED TO
BE A GREAT FRIEND,
I WOULD . . .

BE A
PROMPT
RESPONDER

BE PROMPT WITH RESPONSES, OR YOU MAY FIND YOURSELF MISSING OUT ON THE JOYS OF FRIENDSHIP.

It's an honor when friends go to the trouble of including you in their plans. Whether it's a lunch date or an excursion, they have chosen to spend their time with you.

It's vitally important that you respond promptly to invitations if you want to continue to be included in events, big and small. If you're invited by phone, respond within twenty-four hours, if at all possible, or let friends know when you will have a definite answer for them. If you've received a written invitation, post it in a place where you will see it. Highlight the RSVP date and make sure you respond on time.

Hail, ye small, sweet courtesies of life! For smooth do ye make the road.

LAURENCE STERNE

IF I REALLY WANTED TO
BE A GREAT FRIEND,
I WOULD . . .

NEVER UNDERESTIMATE THE POWER OF A MOVIE

Be moved by a movie.

W hether it's a chick flick, a guy flick, or an oldie flick, movies can be a powerful medium to share with a friend. Movies often express human thoughts, emotions, and common experiences in a vivid way.

Sharing a movie with a friend can be another way of building intimacy—igniting the interchange of thoughts, feelings, and memories. Sometimes movies can express for us what we could not express on our own. Other times they might inspire us to reach toward personal growth and become better people. So take advantage of a night at the movies, and don't forget to bring along a friend to share the laughter, tears, and memories.

There can be no transforming of darkness into light and of apathy into movement without emotion.

Carl Gustav Jung

IF I REALLY WANTED TO
BE A GREAT FRIEND,
I WOULD . . .

DEAL WITH MY EMOTIONAL BAGGAGE

LIGHTEN YOUR LOAD—DROP YOUR BAGGAGE AND PICK UP A FRIEND.

A ll human beings have painful experiences that have an impact on them at some level. These experiences can affect the way we make decisions and relate to others. If you are experiencing feelings of guilt, failure, anger, or even shame as a result of past experiences, don't ignore them. They are likely to intensify, and these feelings will undoubtedly affect your friendships.

It will take some courage, but if you want to be a more secure, loving person and grow in the life and gifts that God has in store for you, it's vital that you work to heal broken places in your heart. Take a look at yourself honestly. Be willing to talk with God, your close friends, or maybe even a professional counselor. The healthier you are emotionally, the healthier your friendships will be.

The first rule is to keep an untroubled spirit. The second is to look things in the face and know them for what they are.

MARCUS AURELIUS

IF I REALLY WANTED TO
BE A GREAT FRIEND,
I WOULD . . .

BE THERE
WHEN THE
CHIPS ARE
DOWN

BE AN ALL-WEATHER FRIEND.

George Eliot wrote, "What do we live for if not to make life less difficult for each other?" Sometimes life can feel like an emotional land mine. We take a few steps and enjoy safety and security, only to take another step and have circumstances blow up around us.

Be a faithful friend when someone is going through a hard time. This can be especially important if your friend is experiencing a loss or disappointment. These sometimes take months, even years, to heal. The true support of a friend can help ease the burden. Your compassion and concern may be what your friend needs to find peace amidst the difficulty. This friend will undoubtedly be with you when you hit a valley of your own.

Carry each others burdens, and in this way you will fulfill the law of Christ.

GALATIANS 6:2

IF I REALLY WANTED TO
BE A GREAT FRIEND,
I WOULD . . .

KEEP A BIRTHDAY CALENDAR

MARK THE YEARS OF LIFE WITH ENTHUSIASM AND FESTIVITY.

Birthdays are important. They are opportunities to celebrate not only the day someone was born but also the beginning of the year ahead. Make a point to find out when your friends' birthdays are and mark them on a calendar. Make sure that you pick out a card or gift, bake a favorite treat, buy flowers, or take your friend out for a special lunch or dinner.

There are even calendars specifically designed to help you remember and acknowledge birthdays. However you decide to honor your friends, they will appreciate your thoughtfulness and feel special on their big day.

We turn not older with the years, but newer with every day.

EMILY DICKINSON

Offer to

Watch

the Kids

FRIENDS DON'T LET FRIENDS GO WITHOUT BREAKS.

Most parents relish an evening out without the kids—an opportunity to reconnect with the adult world. This is doubly true of parents who don't have immediate family living nearby. Consider offering to watch your friends' children on occasion. Some friends find it helpful to trade off now and then to give each other a break.

If you have a strong circle of friends, you can organize a babysitting co-op and establish a rotating schedule of sitting so that you can plan in advance for your nights out. Regardless, you will engender gratefulness and closeness as you seek to meet your friends' needs—and you will help develop friendships among the children too.

Come, dear children, let us away.

MATTHEW ARNOLD

IF I REALLY WANTED TO
BE A GREAT FRIEND,
I WOULD . . .

LOVE
UNCONDITIONALLY

UNCONDITIONAL LOVE INSPIRES LIMITLESS WAYS TO GROW.

Unconditional love is an amazing concept that gives us a sense of worth and freedom in a world that's otherwise filled with reciprocal conditions. Yet when it comes to practicing this super-human virtue, it's none too easy. The characteristics of unconditional love are patience, kindness, humility, and keeping no record of wrongs, to name a few. Unconditional love means accepting and loving people for who they are—faults as well as strengths.

In order to practice unconditional love toward your friends, you must orient yourself in that direction. The words of the Bible, telling us about God's grace and love, and other books of "virtue," both old and new, can inspire you to live a life of love. Friends will know that even with their human frailties, they are safe and secure in their relationship with you.

Above all, love each other deeply.

1 PETER 4:8

IF I REALLY WANTED TO
BE A GREAT FRIEND,
I WOULD . . .

CLIP ARTICLES AND SAVE COUPONS

KEEP YOUR FRIENDS IN MIND FOR THAT SWEET LITTLE FIND!

An easy way to let your friends know that you are thinking of them when you are apart is to clip articles or coupons that might be of interest to them. Keep a coupon envelope handy in your home and in your car. You may even come across a coupon for donuts and coffee or a two-for-one lunch special that you can enjoy with a friend.

Imagine how it would make you feel if someone took the time to clip something of interest to you. Life can become so hectic. If you can take that extra minute to cut the coupon or write a quick note, it could make a lasting difference for a friend.

Friends share all things.

PYTHAGORAS

IF I REALLY WANTED TO
BE A GREAT FRIEND,
I WOULD . . .

SHOW UP
AND SHOW
SUPPORT

Show you care by being there.

If your friend is involved in events, activities, or a specific pursuit (like taking art classes or getting a degree), don't overlook opportunities to show your support. The same goes for your friend's children. This can be such a morale booster for people. It shows you care about what they are involved in and that you want to share in their lives.

If your friend is a speaker, make a point to attend a meeting when he or she is speaking. If their child is in a school play, make a point to attend the show. Share in your friend's feelings of pride and accomplishment and watch your friendship grow as a result.

For kindness begets kindness evermore.

Sophocles

COMMIT TO SPIRITUAL GROWTH

INVEST IN YOUR SOUL AND SHARE THE DIVIDENDS WITH YOUR FRIENDS.

When we have a vital and growing relationship with God, it's usually easier to have vital and growing relationships with others. The Bible gives us wisdom, comfort, and guidance for life's bumpy roads. The more we fill our minds and hearts with God's words, the more secure we become as human beings. We also feel more like reaching out to others when we feel secure within.

Some practical ways to grow spiritually include: attending church and Sunday school, attending a Bible study, reading books, and listening to teaching tapes, worship tapes, and Christian music. When you feed your soul, not only will you grow, but your friendships will too.

The fear of the Lord leads to life: Then one rests content, untouched by trouble.

PROVERBS 19:23

IF I REALLY WANTED TO
BE A GREAT FRIEND,
I WOULD . . .

VERBALIZE MY FEELINGS

What human being on the face of this planet wouldn't love to hear the words, "I love spending time with you!" Everyone desires to be appreciated and affirmed—it's one of the deepest human needs.

If you have a blast when you're with your friends, find yourself growing into a better person because of your friends, or feel like you can totally be yourself with your friends—tell them. Friendships enhance our lives, and those who comprise our friendships need to know how much we value them. You can't say, "I appreciate you," too often to your friends.

To be manifestly loved, to be openly admired are human needs as basic as breathing. Why, then, wanting them so much ourselves do we deny them so often to others?

ARTHUR GORDON

IF I REALLY WANTED TO
BE A GREAT FRIEND,
I WOULD . . .

BE
HONEST

HONESTY, TEMPERED WITH LOVE, IS THE BEST POLICY.

B eing honest with your friends can be tricky. We wonder, "Will I offend if I say what I really feel?" Sometimes it's tough to be honest because we want what we say to be met with approval. Yet most friends, especially those who are secure with themselves, don't want a "yes man" for a buddy.

Assert your opinion—just be certain to temper your honesty with graciousness and tact. If Friday is a more convenient day to meet than Thursday, say so. If you prefer to go to the museum rather than a movie, tell your friend. Once you've expressed how you truly feel about something, then you and your friend can discuss a compromise that suits you both.

A friend is a person with whom I may be sincere. Before him, I may think aloud.

RALPH WALDO EMERSON

BE WILLING TO SHARE THE THINGS THAT MOVE ME

To be known truly, we must reveal truly

In order to build intimacy in a friendship, it's necessary to share things that touch your heart and affect you emotionally or spiritually. If there's a song, quote, book, or movie that has meant a lot to you, share it. Then tell your friend why it's significant to you and how it made you feel or what it made you think about.

Sharing the things that move you creates a point of bonding. It also helps you broaden your friend's perspective. If you hold back your thoughts, feelings, and opinions, there is little chance of deepening communication and learning what motivates and makes up the essence of the other person.

"Out of the overflow of the heart the mouth speaks."

Matthew 12:34

IF I REALLY WANTED TO
BE A GREAT FRIEND,
I WOULD . . .

BE ON TIME

BEING LATE MEANS SOMEONE HAS TO WAIT.

T ry to be on time (or at least within five min-
utes) when you meet your friends. If you tend
to run late, be honest and say, "I tend to run
late, but I want to work on that. Can we have a five- or
ten-minute grace period for our get-togethers?"

Agree to call ahead if you are running late. If you
and your friend have an agreed-upon grace period, as
well as a commitment to call if you're running later, then
each of you can use the time to your advantage rather
than sitting and stewing while you wait, Try a variety
of techniques and gimmicks to help you be a more prompt
friend.

Life is not so short but that there is always time
enough for courtesy.

RALPH WALDO EMERSON

IF I REALLY WANTED TO
BE A GREAT FRIEND,
I WOULD . . .

TRY NOT
TO TAKE
MYSELF TOO
SERIOUSLY

BEING TOO HARD ON YOURSELF CAN MAKE YOU HARD TO BE AROUND.

The more at ease we become with ourselves—shortcomings, quirks, and all—the more other people will be relaxed in our presence. If you flub up in some way, don't take it too seriously. Imitate a duck. The soft, downy feathers underneath the top feathers stay dry and collected, because the top feathers have a special oil that protects the feathers underneath.

To be a good friend, that's how we should respond—calm, cool, collected on the inside, while taking mistakes and embarrassments in stride. If you're confident of God's unconditional love for you, and you have friends who will "roll" with you, you can take life a little less seriously for the sake of those around you.

Enter self-seriousness, exit humor; exit humor, exit sanity.

WILLIAM KIRK KILPATRICK

IF I REALLY WANTED TO
BE A GREAT FRIEND,
I WOULD . . .

LEARN
TO
CELEBRATE

Some people grow up in families where birthday parties and special occasions are always celebrated. Other people grow up in families where birthdays and special occasions are nominally acknowledged. If you grew up in that kind of family, it may take a little extra effort to see how important the art of celebration is.

The word celebrate means "to mark by festivities or deviation from routine." Implicit in the word celebration is the idea that you are stepping away from the normal routine to honor another. When good friends celebrate victories and milestones with each other, it deepens the love and appreciation between them. When you initiate a celebration, it says you're willing to take time out expressly for them.

Rejoice with those who rejoice.

ROMANS 12:15

TRY NOT TO TAKE OTHERS TOO SERIOUSLY

A GOOD FRIEND ROLLS WITH THE PUNCHES.

Part of being a good friend is realizing that everyone has a bad moment or a tough day now and then. And there are always "issues" that pop up spontaneously, rearing their ugly heads and making brief, unexpected appearances.

If your normally bubbly buddy seems to have had some air let out of his bubble, don't take it personally. Most of us have a day when we feel cranky or just plain unhappy. Be a pal and allow for momentary deviations from the norm. Hopefully your friend will do the same for you when you're behavior is not quite up to par.

Afoot and light-hearted I take to the open road.

WALT WHITMAN

IF I REALLY WANTED TO
BE A GREAT FRIEND,
I WOULD . . .

BE TOLERANT OF FAMILY PETS

Remember: To some, pets are people too.

What can you do when you're not a dog lover, but your friend pulls you into a pet, slobber, and romp session with the family Saint Bernard? Friendship does not obligate you to endure pooch exuberance, but absolute intolerance of the pretty pup or the precious kitty can scuttle a friend-ship in a hurry.

If you want to be a great friend, be careful not to make fun of the pet or otherwise dis' the darling. If it's not a big deal for you to pet or compliment the animal in some way—go ahead and do it. And make sure you know the pet's name!

All animals are equal, but some animals are more equal than others.

GEORGE ORWELL

IF I REALLY WANTED TO
BE A GREAT FRIEND,
I WOULD . . .

JOIN A
BIBLE STUDY
GROUP

EARNEST PURSUITS PRODUCE EARNEST FRIENDSHIPS.

Getting involved in a Bible study with a friend allows you to get to know each other in a more meaningful way. A Bible study often provides a setting in which to take conversation below the surface and away from the day's weather.

If you find it challenging to have personal, one-on-one conversations with people, a Bible study can help break the ice and provide some practice in verbalizing important thoughts and feelings—all within a nurturing, affirming environment. Most churches have Bible study groups for all ages and genders. It's a great place to make new friends.

Keep my commands and you will live; guard my teachings as the apple of your eye.

PROVERBS 7:2

IF I REALLY WANTED TO
BE A GREAT FRIEND,
I WOULD . . .

SUGGEST WE MEET AT MY HOUSE

GIVE YOURSELF AN INSTANT HOUSE-WARMING PARTY; INVITE THE GLOW OF FRIENDSHIP.

I nviting someone to your home is a wonderful way to get to know them better and for them to get to know more about you. When you host people in your home, you are revealing your tastes, talents, and your most cherished possessions. Often this will spark a wonderful exchange between you and a potential friend.

Your friends will be reminded of possessions, memories, or photos that have special meaning to them. Often they will begin to share stories or thoughts and feelings that can deepen your understanding of what's important to them. And don't let perfectionistic tendencies about house cleaning hinder you—it's enough to pick up clutter and see that the guest bathroom is presentable.

Happy is the house that shelters a friend.

RALPH WALDO EMERSON

IF I REALLY WANTED TO
BE A GREAT FRIEND,
I WOULD . . .

TREAT SOMEONE TO COFFEE OR TEA

SPOT YOUR FRIENDS A "CUPPA" TEA OR A MUG O' JOE.

The English have an enviable tradition of sharing afternoon tea with friends and family. This is even carried out in some workplaces in England, resulting in happy, more productive workers. What a lovely way to get off of life's carousel for a time to refocus on one of the most important things in life—relationships.

Coffee bars and tea rooms are springing up all over the country, so it's a perfect time to invite a friend to linger with you over a warm, soothing cup of premium coffee or tea. Take time out of your busy day to relax and focus on some heart-to-heart conversation. It will be an investment you won't regret.

Polly; put the kettle on,
We'll all have tea.

NURSERY RHYME

IF I REALLY WANTED TO
BE A GREAT FRIEND,
I WOULD . . .

FOLLOW THROUGH

A PROMISE IS A TERRIBLE THING TO BREAK.

One way to dampen the sparks of friendship is to let someone down by not keeping your word. Don't say yes to a friend and then back-pedal or forget to honor the commitment Adults can be just as disappointed as children when something they were looking forward to doesn't happen, especially when it's due to a careless oversight.

Keep a calendar if you have a tendency to double book or overbook yourself. Keep a wall calendar at home and a small calendar that you can carry with you when you leave the house. Make a point to update (or at least look at!) your calendar each day. Great friends keep their commitments.

"Simply let your 'Yes' be 'Yes', and your 'No', 'No!'"

MATTHEW 5:37

IF I REALLY WANTED TO
BE A GREAT FRIEND,
I WOULD . . .

RESIST THE
URGE TO
BE A
KNOW-IT-ALL

WHEN YOU TOOT YOUR OWN HORN, YOU'RE SOUNDING OFF INSECURITY.

We all have varying levels of knowledge, intelligence, and expertise, but one thing is certain: No one likes to be around someone who is constantly reminding everyone of what they know or can do.

Try an experiment in self-awareness. The next time you're with a friend or in a group of people, listen to what you're saying. Do you have a tendency to validate yourself by bestowing wisdom or knowledge upon those around you? Purpose instead to become a good listener and "questioner" rather than feeling compelled to share your wealth of knowledge. People will grow to respect you, and in time, you may find them clamoring for your input or expertise.

If the best company is that which we leave feeling most satisfied with ourselves, it follows that it is the company we leave most bored.

GIACOMO LEOPARDI

IF I REALLY WANTED TO
BE A GREAT FRIEND,
I WOULD . . .

LEARN HUMILITY

TO KEEP FROM GETTING A FAT HEAD, EAT HUMBLE PIE.

It's human nature to want to be recognized as significant or unique, to have our talents and skills noted by others. But most of us would admit that it's tough to admire someone whose ego precedes him, regardless of how much he or she excels in a particular area.

If you have achievements that you are proud of, let them trickle out as it's appropriate. Don't flaunt your achievements in order to reel in a new friend or two. If you truly are adept in a certain area, over time, friends will notice. Do ask about and acknowledge the achievements of your friends—encouraging and praising others is always in good taste.

Avoid shame, hut do not seek glory—nothing so expensive as glory.

SYDNEY SMITH

VALIDATE
AND
ELEVATE

SEE, HEAR, AND RESPOND WITH THE SENSES OF THE HEART.

Pain, unfortunately, is an inescapable part of being human. Sooner or later, each of your friends will walk through a tough time. If you want to be a great friend, you will be quick to offer support. Remember, no matter how well you know a person, you can't really understand what he or she is feeling unless you've gone through the same experience. The important thing is to *acknowledge* and *validate their feelings.*

After acknowledging the hurt, encourage your friend to take heart. Offer to pray with him or her. And if it's appropriate, help your friend seek the right counsel. Depending on the situation, you may want to suggest a healthy distraction—a movie, hike, or a shopping trip can act as a welcome release.

Encourage one another and build each other up.

1 THESSALONIANS 5:11

IF I REALLY WANTED TO
BE A GREAT FRIEND,
I WOULD . . .

ATTEND SEMINARS AND RETREATS

Retreat for fellowship and friendship.

D o you remember the carefree feeling you had as a child going off to summer camp with a busload of your friends? You can recapture that same sense of anticipation and fun as an adult and strengthen friendships at the same time.

Retreats and seminars provide a relaxed environment away from the routines and responsibilities of daily life. They're natural settings in which to meet new friends or focus on current friendships. Often the theme of a retreat or seminar provides a built in "connection" among those in attendance. Everyone is hearing and reflecting on the same inspiring or challenging information. This can lead to meaningful conversation that helps deepen friendships.

How dear to this heart are the scenes of my childhood.

Samuel Woodworth

IF I REALLY WANTED TO
BE A GREAT FRIEND,
I WOULD . . .

SEIZE THE DAY

MAKE TODAY COUNT, TOMORROW IS NEVER A CERTAINTY.

At some point, most of us have returned from a funeral thinking, "Life is so short. I need to make the most of it." But too quickly we fall back into our routines and ruts and don't truly appreciate the moments we have or live each one to its fullest.

If an event or play is coming to town that gets your heart pumping or your feet dancing with anticipation—call a friend and make plans to go. Events and plays move on to other towns and sometimes unexpectedly, your friends do too. Accidents, illnesses, and the need to take care of an ill family member can pop up unexpectedly, so seize the day while you have the opportunity and health to do so.

Yesterday is history, tomorrow is a mystery, today is a gift—that's why it's the present.

ANONYMOUS

IF I REALLY WANTED TO
BE A GREAT FRIEND,
I WOULD . . .

RESIST THE URGE TO BE A FIXER

HOUSEHOLD APPLIANCES NEED REPAIRMEN—FRIENDS DON'T.

In our "get it quick" society, where we are used to having many needs and wants met almost instantaneously, it's easy to want to fix our friends' problems quickly in order to ease their anxiety. It's a temptation to try to come up with a one-step, easy-fix-it plan.

Often, what our friends need the most is not a pat answer but a shoulder to lean on. Remind yourself that you are being of invaluable help by simply listening. Sometimes people have the right answers locked inside of them. They just need some time to talk to an attentive friend, who may ask intuitive questions, in order to achieve the needed clarity.

It is an honour for a man to cease from strife:
but every fool will be meddling.

PROVERBS 20:3 KJV

IF I REALLY WANTED TO
BE A GREAT FRIEND,
I WOULD . . .

SAVE
THE
SERMONS

SAVE THE SERMON—LIVE IT.

What we believe is a big part of who we are. In the context of friendship, it is almost certain that you will want to share your faith at some point. When the time comes, it's important to be sensitive to the pressure this can put on a friendship.

Differing viewpoints can lead to interesting discussions and help broaden or redefine peoples' perspectives, and that can make a relationship richer. But such a sensitive area should be approached carefully and respectfully. A friend shouldn't feel like he or she is your personal conversion project. As you build a relationship based on mutual love and respect, you will find many opportunities to share the deepest and most precious elements of your faith.

Logic and sermons never convince.

WALT WHITMAN

CREATE A SAFE PLACE TO SHARE IDEAS

IDEAS CAN BE DIAMONDS IN THE ROUGH.

D o you remember how it felt when you were a child and you drew a picture or made something and presented it to someone? Oftentimes we as adults still have that heart-pounding experience when we're sharing an idea with someone. Our minds warn us, "They may not like it!" But something in our spirit yearns to take a risk and share the idea. It's a matter of trust.

Maybe one of your friends has an idea for a creative or meaningful get-together, an easier way to accomplish something, or a small business idea. Make them feel safe by encouraging them to share their ideas—half the fun is *talking and dreaming!*

An invasion of armies can be resisted, but not an idea whose time has come.

VICTOR HUGO

FORGIVE AND ACCEPT FORGIVENESS

ROLL WITH LIFE'S PUNCHES AND GATHER NO MOSS ALONG THE WAY.

If someone has offended you, it's best to either talk with them or forget about it. Don't harbor bitterness by thinking, "They should realize the error of their ways!" Your friend may have no idea that you were offended by something he or she did or did not do.

Remind yourself of the good times, love, and laughter that you have shared with your friend. We all make mistakes, and sometimes we make them more often than we care to admit. In this imperfect world, it's best to learn to roll with the punches, taking disappointments and irritations in stride. The chances are good that your friend will do the same for you.

Love . . . keeps no record of wrongs.

1 CORINTHIANS 13:4-5

IF I REALLY WANTED TO
BE A GREAT FRIEND,
I WOULD . . .

OVERCOME MY FEAR OF MAKING A MISTAKE

MISTAKES ARE THE SEEDLINGS OF FUTURE SUCCESSES.

Nobody likes to make mistakes—but everybody makes them. What separates growing, optimistic people from the rest of the pack is that they aren't afraid of their mistakes. They don't wallow in them. They look at a mistake and ask themselves two questions, "What went wrong?" and "How do I avoid making the same mistake again?"

Most people are more forgiving and less petty than we think. After all—we're only human. If you're late to meet a friend for a date or if you let a comment slip from your lips that you wish you hadn't—just say you're sorry. Then let it go and keep moving forward.

A man of genius makes no mistakes. His errors are volitional and are the portals of discovery.

JAMES JOYCE

IF I REALLY WANTED TO
BE A GREAT FRIEND,
I WOULD . . .

REFRAIN FROM BORROWING MONEY

VALUE YOUR FRIENDSHIP? DON'T PUT ANY VALUE BETWEEN IT.

It can be tempting, when finances get tight, to ask a friend for help. In rare circumstances, this might work out—especially if you are absolutely certain that you will be able to repay the money within a few weeks.

If you are unable to pay your friend back quickly, you may invite negative issues into your friendship—even in a good, secure, and long-standing relationship. Your friend may begin to doubt that you are trustworthy if you can't repay the loan as quickly as you said. Or one or the other of you may taint the relationship with a perceived sense of obligation. Think long and hard before allowing money to become a wedge in your friendship.

The holy passion of Friendship is of so sweet and steady and loyal and enduring a nature that it will last through a whole lifetime, if not asked to lend money.

MARK TWAIN

BE NICE
TO MY
FRIENDS'
FAMILIES

ALWAYS KEEP YOUR FRIEND'S FAMILY IN YOUR PERIPHERAL VISION.

Don't forget that spouses and kids are a huge part of your friends' lives, if they have them. The adage, "Love me—love my family!" is a good one to keep in mind. Make sure you greet your friends' family members when they come into the room. Ask a couple of questions like, "How's that soccer team doing?" or "How's your new job going?"

On occasion, consider giving something to the family or a particular family member, whether it's a belonging of yours or a baked good to share. Extending courtesy and kindness toward your friends' family members will touch your friends' hearts and endear you to them.

God setteth the solitary in families.

PSALM 68:6 KJV

IF I REALLY WANTED TO
BE A GREAT FRIEND,
I WOULD . . .

SHARE THE BEAUTY OF NATURE

SHARE SUNSETS AND SEASONS WITH SOMEONE SPECIAL.

God has made some amazing things! Sometimes we get blinded to the beauty of creation because we are so focused on the routines of daily life. Make a point to get out and reacquaint yourself with God's incomparable creativity. Ask a friend to join you on a walk or accompany you to a park, lake, or botanical garden. Notice the flowers, trees, birds, and squirrels. Take in the sights, sounds, and smells.

Sharing nature with a friend can be a wonderfully relaxing and invigorating experience. When you get back to your daily routines, you may find yourself daydreaming about that lovely day you spent with your friend and making mental notes about where to go next!

Apprentice yourself to nature. Not a day will pass without her opening a new and wondrous world of experience to learn from and enjoy.

RICHARD W. LANGER

If I really wanted to
Be a Great Friend,
I would . . .

Get a Sense of Humor

LAUGH YOUR WAY INTO YOUR FRIENDS' HEARTS.

A good sense of humor is an immeasurable source of joy when shared with friends. Tossing around comedic insights about this crazy life can foster a lighthearted atmosphere that will bring energy into your friendships.

If a good sense of humor does not come naturally to you, there are ways to cultivate one. Train your brain to be observant during conversations. You may find that something someone says triggers a funny memory or a play on words. Observe people who have a good sense of humor and note how they interject humor into everyday life and conversation. The important thing is to make an honored place for shared laughter among friends.

Among those whom I like or admire, I can find no common denominator, but among those whom I love, I can: all of them make me laugh.

W. H. AUDEN

REFUSE TO "USE" MY FRIENDS

Refrain from being a bait-and-switch friend.

Have you ever been invited to a friend's house or to a church function only to realize you were invited in order to introduce you to a business opportunity or ask you to volunteer for something? Most of us resent these kinds of experiences because it feels like we've become an unwitting participant in a game of "bait and switch."

When it comes to friendship, good friends don't mix business with pleasure. Make sure you don't invite people to your home or other events on false pretenses. If you head up a volunteer area of a church or school, don't imply that you're looking for friendship when you're really looking for volunteers.

Let love be without hypocrisy.

Romans 12:9 NKJV

IF I REALLY WANTED TO
BE A GREAT FRIEND,
I WOULD . . .

LOOK
AT THE
LIGHT SIDE

WHEN IT'S LAUGH OR CRY, THE CHOICE IS CLEAR. LAUGH UNTIL YOU SHED A TEAR!

L ife at times can feel overwhelming, painful, and very serious. There are so many elements in our lives that we cannot control. It's easy to become anxious and lose our joy.

But even in the midst of tough times, when we find ourselves saying, "It's laugh or cry," laughter can be therapeutic. We can literally feel stress escaping from our bodies as we let loose a belly laugh (possibly even laughing to the point of tears!). Maybe the problem hasn't gone away but some of the anxiety has, and we find a cleansing property in a good laugh that helps us get up and keep going.

With the fearful strain that is on me night and day, if I did not laugh I should die.

ABRAHAM LINCOLN

IF I REALLY WANTED TO
BE A GREAT FRIEND,
I WOULD . . .

SEEK OUT SELF-IMPROVEMENT

One of the best and quickest ways to expand your personal horizons, as well as strengthen a friendship, is to join a club or take a class with a friend. Sharing a common interest can build a strong bond between people in a short time.

Search your heart and ask yourself what kinds of things you really care about and want to learn more about. The more your heart is into the club, class, or cause, the more likely you will be to stick with it. In time, gifts and talents will begin to emerge and be shared between you and your friend, deepening and renewing your relationship.

Every day; in every way; I'm getting better and better.

ÉMILE COUÉ

IF I REALLY WANTED TO
BE A GREAT FRIEND,
I WOULD . . .

STOP TALKING

Good conversations that hold the interest of both parties should resemble a good passing game in basketball. No one should hold on to the ball of conversation very long before passing it to another teammate.

Become aware of how much "air time" you are occupying in a conversation. Suppress the tendency to reveal your life story and unique experiences in a few conversations. Pace yourself. Remind yourself that there will be opportunities in the future to reveal who you are and the things you have done. It's important to remember to invite conversation from your friend. Be more interested in learning about them than you are in having them learn about you.

Everyone should be quick to listen, slow to speak.

JAMES 1:19

IF I REALLY WANTED TO
BE A GREAT FRIEND,
I WOULD . . .

GIVE FLOWERS, PLANTS, OR FRESH FRUIT

Be a fresh, fragrant friend.

Flowers, plants, and fresh fruit add color and fragrance to a room and invoke feelings of tranquility when displayed within the home. What a terrific and inexpensive way to treat your friends to something special on an otherwise ordinary day. If you have a garden, home-grown vegetables are always a treat.

Keep a supply of inexpensive vases and baskets on hand to make it easier to quickly arrange some fruit, flowers, or a plant to give away. Gifts of this nature are a wonderful way to let your friends know you are thinking of them. And they will no doubt be thinking warm thoughts about you each time they see your earthy gift.

Flowers are lovely; love is flower-like; friendship is a sheltering tree.

Samuel Taylor Coleridge

IF I REALLY WANTED TO
BE A GREAT FRIEND,
I WOULD . . .

USE MY PHONE TO STAY IN TOUCH

YOUR FIVE-MINUTE CALL CAN MAKE SOMEONE'S TWENTY-FOUR HOURS.

I f you, like most people, are an on-the-go person with a full schedule, you may want to make use of your phone to help you stay connected with your friends. It's amazing what a day can bring—good or bad. A wonderful way to be a caring friend is to check on your friends occasionally.

If you have a cell phone, make use of any "down time" you have while driving, waiting at airports, or waiting in line. Call a friend and let him or her know you care about how things are going in their daily life.

How you call to me, call to me.

THOMAS HARDY

SEEK
OUT A
MENTOR

SEEK OUT A MENTOR TO HELP YOU NAVIGATE LIFE'S CHALLENGES.

A mentoring friendship is one in which someone who has been through similar life experiences can be an empathetic shoulder to lean on and an encouraging coach to help us navigate life's challenges.

Generally speaking, experience comes with age, and wisdom comes from experience. If you know of someone who has been through some of the life passages you are facing, ask them if they might have the time to share with you over lunch or coffee. Don't be discouraged if your first choice does not have the time or interest in a mentoring friendship. Keep praying for the right match to come along.

The older women . . . can train the younger women.

TITUS 2:3-4

IF I REALLY WANTED TO
BE A GREAT FRIEND,
I WOULD . . .

SMILE
AT
PILES

EASY-TO-BE-WITH FRIENDS "SMILE AT PILES."

Many people have "piles" in their houses. Often these are stacks of mail, school papers, or pictures that haven't made it into drawers or albums yet. You may often hear, "Please don't look at my piles!" when you visit someone's home. Just smile and say, "Relax, I have piles too, and so do most of my friends."

Inviting someone into your home—with its subtle or obvious imperfections—can be an act of vulnerability. This can be especially true for neat-nicks, who are never satisfied with the condition of their homes, or for those who feel they lack a knack for decorating. What's most important is working (or chilling out) to make your friends feel at ease.

I am little concerned with beauty or perfection.

EMILE ZOLA

IF I REALLY WANTED TO
BE A GREAT FRIEND,
I WOULD . . .

BE CAREFUL
NOT TO
HOLD ON
TOO TIGHT

There's a rubber-band effect in most friendships —a coming together and a pulling back at times. Don't be afraid of this dynamic. Some weeks may be more hectic than usual for a friend, and there may be times of physical and emotional exhaustion.

Feel free to check on your friend if you haven't been in touch as often as usual, but don't take it personally if your friend needs a little time and space to navigate things in his or her life or heart. A good friend will do the same for you; and when the time is right, he or she just might share something about slowing down and coming to a place of personal realization or emotional healing.

The fastest way to lose love is to hold it too tightly; and the best way to keep it is to give it wings.

NANCY SIMS

IF I REALLY WANTED TO
BE A GREAT FRIEND,
I WOULD . . .

AFFIRM
POSSIBILITY
THINKING

A FRIEND ENCOURAGES THE DREAMS OF THE HEART.

"You did it!" Who doesn't love to hear those sweet words of success? Seek to give the gift of encouragement to your friend's aspirations. Resist the urge to be a naysayer. Oftentimes all a person needs is a friend to say, "Go for it!" in order to pursue a dream that's been simmering in his or her heart for a long time.

Leave the results to God. Maybe your friend will follow a few rabbit trails along the way, or in time, he or she may find that a clearer goal has emerged and switch trails altogether. Either way, can you imagine the shared joy of standing with your friend at the finish line and saying, "You did it!"

"With God all things are possible."

MATTHEW 19:26

IF I REALLY WANTED TO
BE A GREAT FRIEND,
I WOULD . . .

THINK
LONG
TERM

WHEN CONSIDERING YOUR FRIENDSHIPS, CLING TO BIG-PICTURE PERSPECTIVE.

Most relationships become stronger over time due to shared joys, sorrows, hours of conversation, and common life experiences. Don't fret it if a friendship isn't deepening as quickly as you would like. This particular friendship might be a marathon runner instead of a sprinter.

It's easy to lose perspective on time. Think back to the many times throughout your life when you were waiting for something you really desired to happen. At the time it may have seemed like an eternity. But it came at last, and now you barely remember the wait. Good friendships are worth waiting for.

Seven years would be insufficient to make some people acquainted with each other, and seven days are more than enough for others.

JANE AUSTEN

IF I REALLY WANTED TO
BE A GREAT FRIEND,
I WOULD . . .

NEVER UNDERESTIMATE THE POWER OF PROXIMITY

Proximity fosters closeness.

Because of the development of the automobile, the telephone, and now the Internet, people who live many miles apart can still maintain friendships with relative ease. Although "across town" friendships can work, they take much more effort. If both friends aren't committed to overcoming the logistics of distance, it's likely that one will tire of always being the person to make the drive.

Neighborhood friendships or friendships with people who live near places you frequent have a built-in chance of thriving. In a society where many have lost a true sense of community, it's comforting and natural to make friends with neighbors.

Better is a neighbor that is near than a brother far off.

Proverbs 27:10 kjv

ALLOW FOR SEASONS OF FRIENDSHIP

A WINTER IN FRIENDSHIP CAN BLOSSOM INTO A GLOWING SPRING.

Friends come and go for all kinds of reasons: moving, busyness, divorce, illness, or personal transition. Sometimes friends "grow apart" and meet other friends, develop new interests, or they withdraw in a time of difficulty or change. Any of these things can weaken, or even end, a friendship.

Sometimes God allows the paths of our lives and hearts to cross for a season. If this happens, don't fret and don't regret. Be thankful that you were able to share part of your life with someone you really enjoyed. Realize, too, that some friendships develop quickly and others take more time, so be open to the pace that God allows.

The season when to come, and when to go, to sing, or cease to sing, we never know.

Alexander Pope

IF I REALLY WANTED TO
BE A GREAT FRIEND,
I WOULD . . .

MINIMIZE
DISTRACTIONS

MINIMIZE DISTRACTIONS AND MAXIMIZE INTERACTION.

A lmost everyone can relate to being in someone's office and having a conversation interrupted by a phone call. You feel like an eavesdropper, twiddling your thumbs while the person on the phone takes precedence. This same situation often occurs in the home around friends. What message does this send?

Children can also be a great distraction. When conversing with a friend, make it clear that the children are not to interrupt unless it's important. Under most circumstances, try to minimize distractions and send a message that you are giving your friend the gift of time —unhurried, undivided, and uninterrupted.

Do you know that conversation is one of the greatest pleasures in life? But it wants leisure.

WILLIAM SOMERSET MAUGHAM

IF I REALLY WANTED TO
BE A GREAT FRIEND,
I WOULD . . .

TAKE CARE OF MY BODY

WHEN YOU FEEL GOOD, YOU'LL FEEL GOOD ABOUT GIVING ENERGY TO FRIENDSHIPS TOO.

D o you notice when you're tired or in need of a refreshing break or soothing shower that *nothing* seems very interesting or exciting? It's hard to be a loving, giving person when your "self" is dog tired. However, when you feel physically rested and fit, you will have more energy to give to a vital lifestyle and flourishing friendships.

In addition to regular exercise, make sure you get enough nightly rest, and take time to relax. Friends who are constantly stressed usually don't make the best kind of friends. A lifestyle of unending stress is not conducive to building friendships, so take inventory and make adjustments as necessary.

Do you not know that your body is a temple of the Holy Spirit?

1 CORINTHIANS 6:19

IF I REALLY WANTED TO
BE A GREAT FRIEND,
I WOULD . . .

BE CAREFUL NOT TO PUT ALL MY EGGS IN ONE BASKET

BE A SMART INVESTOR IN FRIENDSHIPS—DIVERSIFY YOUR PORTFOLIO.

I n His unfathomable wisdom and creativity, God made us all different! This is an exciting and fulfilling aspect of making several good friends. No one friend can meet all your friendship needs all the time.

Don't put all your eggs (friendship needs) in one basket. Try to develop at least three or four good friendships over time. Embrace the idea that each friend is uniquely special—just like the varied colors and designs of hand-dyed Easter eggs in a wicker basket. You will find all of your friendships are more satisfying when you have a variety of friends that you can call upon to share a range of activities.

Variety's the very spice of life.

WILLIAM COWPER

IF I REALLY WANTED TO
BE A GREAT FRIEND,
I WOULD . . .

WATCH MY TONGUE

KEEP AN EYE ON YOUR TONGUE, AND AN EAR PEELED FOR WHAT IT IS SAYING.

It's a bad feeling when we let something slip from our lips that we wish we hadn't said. Words are a powerful form of communication. Not only are words important, but how we say them is just as important. Be observant of the power of your words. Listen for the inflections you use. Try to become aware of your facial expressions and body language as you communicate.

Read materials about the power of speech. In this hectic, stressful world, almost everyone can use a reminder from the pages of a Chinese menu: Flavor your speech a little more sweet and a little less sour.

The tongue has the power of life and death,
and those who love it will eat its fruit.

PROVERBS 18:21

IF I REALLY WANTED TO
BE A GREAT FRIEND,
I WOULD . . .

PACE MYSELF

CARVE OUT TIME FOR THOSE WHO MAKE UP THE GREATEST PART OF YOUR LIFE.

Why is it that we make friends? Often it is for companionship and encouragement in a life filled with uncertainties. If you value friendships but find yourself without enough time to foster and nurture them, you may need to take a look at your time/relationship ratio.

Making room in your life for friendship is a commitment. If you value someone, but your schedule only allows for infrequent visits, let the person know and discuss your situation. Discover expectations, and then decide if they can be met. Abraham Lincoln said that friendships comprise the greatest part of one's life.

If a man does not make new acquaintances as he advances through life, he will soon find himself left alone.

SAMUEL JOHNSON